Volume 107 of the Yale Series of Younger Poets

# *Westerly*

## WILL SCHUTT

Foreword by Carl Phillips

Yale

**UNIVERSITY PRESS**

New Haven and London

Published with assistance from the foundation established in memory of
Amasa Stone Mather of the Class of 1907, Yale College.

Published with assistance from a grant to honor James Merrill.

Yale University Press books may be purchased in quantity for educational,
business, or promotional use. For information, please e-mail
sales.press@yale.edu (U.S. office) or sales@yaleup.co.uk (U.K. office).

Designed by Sonia Shannon.
Set in Bulmer type by Keystone Typesetting, Inc.
Printed in the United States of America.

Library of Congress Cataloging-in-Publication Data
Schutt, Will, 1981–. Westerly / Will Schutt ; foreword by Carl Phillips.
    p.    cm. — (Yale series of younger poets ; v. 107)
Includes bibliographical references.
Poems.
ISBN 978-0-300-18850-9 (cloth : alk. paper)
ISBN 978-0-300-18851-6 (pbk. : alk. paper)
I. Phillips, Carl, 1959–. II. Title.
PS3619.C48335W47 2013
811′.6—dc23
2012033923

A catalogue record for this book is available from the British Library.

This paper meets the requirements of ANSI/NISO Z39.48-1992
(Permanence of Paper).

10 9 8 7 6 5 4 3 2 1

*For Tania—who came west*

Goodbye to the living place, and all I ask it to do is stay alive.

—JAMES WRIGHT

# Contents

# Foreword

Westerly. The word has a doubleness to it, meaning both *toward* the west, and *from* that direction. The west, of course, as also the land of the dead in many traditions—Christian, Homeric, Sumerian among them. Will Schutt's *Westerly* takes on nothing less than—on one hand—the ways in which we the living, both late and soon, make our stumbling way westward, mostly oblivious to the fact of mortality, like the summer people in the book's opening poem; having weathered a storm, they

> walked their drinks down
> to the beach—the happy human chain—
> each tethered to one spot, each for now alive.

And on the other hand, Schutt is mindful of how the dead make their resonant way back to us, sometimes as memory, sometimes as guide directing us toward and through the inevitable. Here's how the book softly ends:

> . . . some narrow sickness buried you.
> Whatever boyhood I had
> fate hijacked too. Old friend, is this that
> world we stayed awake all night for?
> Truth dropped in. Far off,
> your cool hand points the way.

As with the human cycle itself, *Westerly* begins, then, in life, and ends in death. In between, the poems concern youth (the too-soon loss of it), heritage, and that life in particular that gets called privileged: people with summer houses; world travelers for whom towels aren't just red, they're Testarossa red (as in the Ferrari); speakers like the one in "Fragment from a Coptic Tunic," who has the leisure to speculate about "what the salvo of utter faith feels like" as he skims an article about a massacre/martyrdom in Cairo, feeling only a "slightly dull/sensation"; and, in "Golden State Sublet," college kids whose station estranges them from those "beneath" them even as it makes them long for danger, a longing that only the privileged tend to get to enjoy. In that poem, a group of young men become fascinated with two call girls who also live in the building, the men "wanting to fuck them but afraid of the clap," listening to the women fighting until the fighting gets physical, whereupon the men—boys, really—get more than they'd bargained for: that is, they begin to see that not everything is amusing, and much of life is ugly, horrifying, a "blunt *thunk*/you [can't] shake out of your ears."

Which is to say that, like Nick Carraway, Fitzgerald's narrator in *The Great Gatsby* (a book with whose sensibility *Westerly* very much seems in conversation), Schutt sees through the initial glamour of certain lives, to the complexity that lies past that. "We live so strangely," he says at one point, "in love with visions, / scared of the invisible" ("Flywheel with Variable Inertia"). Fear of what's invisible, but clearly real, seems the reason, here, for our need for visions, as if the latter might stall—or distract—us from having to face what's difficult. Hence the "polite fictions / families invent" (in "American Window Dressing"), as a way of avoiding harder truths. Hence the preference for hiding behind the past, rather than wrestling with present identity:

—After my father died I grew
my father's beard. I could carry him

around with me and not some
hunger to be my own man.

And hence the father whose legacy is a clipped language that
resists any revelation of the interior life:

"Put everything into it." My father's
words on Sunday visits. Man of few words.

That's how Schutt's speaker puts it, showing—slyly, comically—
how much of his father he has in fact inherited, though one
doubts that the speaker himself even understands this or, indeed
—heritage again—would know how to say so.

Family, with its polite fictions, its refusal (or inability) to articu-
late reality—that's one part of heritage. Another part with which
Schutt seems especially concerned is that of estrangement, the
ways in which, as we get older, we become more estranged, it
seems, not only from others but from ourselves—who we were,
who we remember being, or what we think we remember, which is
different from knowing. With regard to knowing, there's an in-
triguing passage at the end of Schutt's "From a Middle Distance"
where he's describing a detail from the Velázquez painting *Las
Meninas*:

the narrow
face of a rousing mastiff
whose dark narrow eyes betray
knowing, which is to say restraint.

Restraint as a form—as the confirmation—of knowing: for many
readings of this manuscript, I thought that by restraint Schutt
meant something like reticence, temperance, the sense of grace
and control that informs the poems and their sensibility through-

out *Westerly*. Only later did I come to the more obvious (given the dog) kind of restraint that a leash can be, including the invisible leash by which, whether through patient discipline and training, or worse, through cruelty, the master keeps his dog under control. When is knowledge a thing to be strived for, and when does too much knowledge become crippling, leaving us fixed, mute, and waiting to be told what to do next?

These questions hover over Schutt's elegant translations which, positioned squarely in the middle, seem at once to inform *Westerly*'s sensibility and to be informed by it. What the translations themselves have in common, besides all being from Italian poets who flourished mid-twentieth century, is that their speakers are existentially stymied: "I cannot dissolve into life," says Merini, while the Sanguineti pieces—in style and in content—stutter their way around an ordinariness that blurs into nothingness. And yet Merini believes also in "a sign of coming charity," in going "out to meet my promise"; and for all his concern with nothingness, Sanguineti is not without purpose: "we're kind of trying / to write the complete works of humankind, all of us, together, deep down . . ." Finally, there's the Montale piece, dominated by a rain that falls on everything and everyone, relentlessly, stoppable only by a "you" addressed at poem's end—the intimacy, the human contact that makes our sense of otherwise estrangement bearable?

This certainly seems a theme that gets reinforced in *Westerly*'s final section. Against estrangement, Forster's "only connect," the stranger overheard phoning home ("Strange Giraffe"), saying "I can hear you, can you hear me?" The silent communion at the end of "Elba Journal":

> On my way to piss,
> I spy a boy swallowed in the husk

of his hammock. The spirit, though we make it
otherwise, isn't complicated, rising
and falling in its calligraphic exhaustion.

Or the intimacy that not even death can sever, in "After *A Silvia*,"
where the speaker, addressing his lost friend, remembering "the
hopeful pitch" that governed their past, says:

To think of that time tightens my chest
and grief ploughs through me.

Yet Schutt speaks earlier (in "Beauty Spot") of

                    pain and happiness, which in many
          people's books make beauty.

That would appear to be the case with *Westerly*. Not only beauty
but a persuasive insight into what I call the lived life, the one that
risks knowing what's difficult, despite the sorrow that so often
follows the knowing.

                    The past, in hindsight, appears
          clearly, riddled with wrong measurements.
                                             STRANGE GIRAFFE

Yes. The poems here are quiet, meditative, wry, steeped in know-
ing, and therefore brave. They know our lives are mostly ordi-
nary, lives in which

                    nirvana is a long time
          coming, or untidy, unresolved,
          the way stupid hope won't shut up.

Hard to say whether that *stupid* is meant angrily, ruefully, or
affectionately, like a punch in the arm between friends. Maybe all

three, in a way. "So we beat on, boats against the current, borne
back ceaselessly into the past." Fitzgerald again. But Schutt also.
For maybe the poems do regret the hope that can lead us falsely.
And maybe it's also the case that

> It all starts
> with shame and want, I think, and ends
> in shamelessness and want not.

WILD HOGS

(Does it? Must it?) But even so, Schutt also knows that hope is
what carries us, sustains us, as we pass westward, which may feel
like forward motion, but if toward the dead, who are the past
itself, then what? *Westerly* is in this particular regard a book of
uncommon wisdom, these days especially. The poems seem the
records that Schutt mentions in "Rock Maple, White Pine":

> objects in history's logbook:

> what in the end we ate, drank,
> jarred, girded, anchored and housed.

And so much more than that. The poems sustain me. They give
me hope—which may very well be, among gifts, the one we need
most.

Carl Phillips

# Acknowledgments

Grateful acknowledgment is made to the editors of the following publications, where many of these poems, sometimes in different form, first appeared:

*Agni:* "[what do you do?]"
*Blackbird:* "Apparitions and Incarnations," "Postcard of Peter Lorre Embracing Lotte Lenya, 1929"
*Cimarron Review:* "Fragment from a Coptic Tunic"
*Drunken Boat:* "[one writes especially]"
*FIELD:* "Elba Journal," "Forgetting Waukesha, Remembering St. Helena," "From a Middle Distance," "Strange Giraffe"
*The Hollins Critic:* "We Didn't Start the Fire," "Wild Hogs"
*Kenyon Review Online:* "Beauty Spot," "Transparent Window on a Complex View"
*The Literary Review:* "After *A Silvia*," "A Kind of Poetry," "American Window Dressing"
*Narrative:* "Beach Lane"
*The Southern Review:* "Crenellated Playroom," "The Farther Veil"

I am grateful to the Stadler Center for Poetry at Bucknell University and the James Merrill House for residencies that made the completion of this book possible. Thanks also to the Dorothy Sargent Rosenberg Memorial Fund for generous financial support.

Thanks to the following people for their encouragement and tutelage over the years: Pam Alexander, Danny Anderson, T. J. Anderson III, Paula Closson Buck, Kelly Cherry, Andrew Ciotola, Anna Coda Nunziante, Martha Collins, Martha Cooley, Alfred Corn, Chris Deweese, R. H. W. Dillard, Miriam Grottanelli, Cathryn Hankla, Luke Johnson, Shara McCallum, Thorpe Moeckel, Mike Scalise, Eric Trethewey, G. C. Waldrep, and David Young.

Many thanks to Carl Phillips for his gentle but firm stewardship.

Thanks to my father for his patient advocacy.

And to my mother for her superb example.

# We Didn't Start the Fire

Two doors down lived a descendant of de Sade.
    He rode a vintage Trek in a gingham shirt.
A blue Hamsa strung around his neck
        waved when he waved. The name meant
nearly nil to us, cluelessly humming the catalog
        of history in "We Didn't Start the Fire"—
*Harry Truman, Ho Chi Minh, Rockefeller, Roy Cohn.*
        Hunting arrowheads, we made off with a haul
of tangled wires, nickeled tubs. Some inheritance.
        *Children of thalidomide, hypodermics on the shore.*
Between the cemetery and schoolhouse
        rows of thuja formed a buffer. Most headstones
looked as if an animal had rubbed his back
        up and down against them. Most hurricanes
amounted to little more than steady drizzle.
        Townies spray-painted the bridge: "Sayonara,
Bob" or "Safe travels, Sucker." At sunset
        summer people walked their drinks down
to the beach—the happy human chain—
        each tethered to one spot, each for now alive.

# Golden State Sublet

The unfurnished third-floor walk-up
slept four to a room. We dropped our bags
on the deep padding of the brand new
cut and loop carpet and called it a night.
Another summer we'd be sleeping elsewhere.
Each morning kids from Heroica
Nogales or Zacatecoluca or whatever the hell
the oven was they'd shimmied up out of
went door-to-door hawking loaves of bread
their mothers had baked for a buck
while their fathers hit the curb till sundown,
then wandered back, work or no work,
stopping most of the night on the stairwell.
The rims of their big, far-off, lacquered eyes
shuttered up as we stepped over them.
Unlike their fathers, the kids sank a hook in you
with their eyes so that it was harder to say
"*No, gracias, nada,*" wheel around them
and head off for a dollop of egg fooyung
at the Dollar Chinese or corn grilled
husk-on and served right out in the glare
of the pavement with a lump of paprika
mayonnaise and a wedge of lime. Night after night
a waitress netted our dinner from a fish tank
crowded with bright gorgonian polyp.

Surfing had been the whole point
of that summer, *some maundering fancy of going
out with the tide.* We took turns with a book
about Jack London's trip to Hawaii
before he dropped dead at Beauty Ranch.
Beauty Ranch, the name seemed so American,
the rough and smooth ends of it
elbowing each other out, how ranch stuck
a muzzle on beauty. We called the silent
afternoon sprawl of the ocean "Pluto Zilch,"
sitting westward way out beyond the breakers—
the one way we knew nothing
would drag us under, and we could sit very still
with the big sun fleecing our chests
and maybe catch a glimpse of Guadalupe
fur seals before somebody paddled by.
"Sit there all you like, at some point
you pussies are going to get pummeled."

That August two pretty peroxide blond
call girls moved in. One was hiding
from her husband. The other was company.
"Gringo Pimps," they called us.
"Here for a laugh?" We just stood back,
wanting to fuck them but afraid of the clap.
We used to lie very still at night
hoping to hear their voices through the wall.
One night we heard the girls beat each other up.
It seemed harmless enough at first.
Mock screaming. A few halfhearted slaps.

Then a sudden, blunt *thunk*
you couldn't shake out of your ears.
Then the awful, dumb, protracted silence.
We lay very still in our room, one
ear in the air, another against the carpet.

# Fragment from a Coptic Tunic

They draped it over the dead.
      That's how it survived
(frayed, mealy, spotted)
         as a language 10% of the population
speaks inside a temple
            survives on the outskirts of a slum.
Spanish, Hindu, Arabic,
         Greek, each museumgoer's headset
murmurs in the room.
         Last week, twenty-six
Christians were shot in Cairo.
         Neighbors marched the corpses
through the streets, their shirts
         pursed in the heat or parted
by a strange wind. I wonder
         what the salvo of utter faith feels like
compared with the slightly dull
         sensation I get, skimming half
the story ("shock—surprise—
         anger"), squaring the paper
("interim—uprising—alongside—
         against") and planting it in my pocket
like a curved blade in a sheath.

## Transparent Window on a Complex View

Brilliant lemon morning. Tania outside
dumping mulch. Two doorstop snowshoe
hares by the door: winter morphs with ferruginous
scuff on their ears. Set on dishcloths,
they're a mix of iron sconce and birch bark.
Honey bunch in the garden. On the sill
a Ziploc bag of permanently wet radicchio
we bought at the farmer's market
from kids in Carhartts who return each year
to tend the horse-powered farm. Apostolic
boredom in their silent straight mouths,
they listen to the chef from the Mexican restaurant
called El El Frijoles sautéing Quorn in soy sauce
and talking up the nutritional value of imitation meat.
Yuma Yellow, the light outside. An unlikely
favorite. Not mine. Fairfield Porter's.
He failed to jump some railroad tracks in a car
that color. To him, what was solid was miraculous:
planes of light, day-old eggs on a white dish,
objects taken frankly by the hour on their own.
No one is especially pretty or monstrous
posed on his lupine and dandelion couch:
Running socks. A red hat. A rocking horse.
That which was real, and changing, and light.

# Beach Lane

It's a tunnel of sorts. They're all tunnels, I guess,
even Further Lane and Muchmore Drive,
which would have us believe beyond the sagging
split-rail fence lies the answer to an urban
dream. Not everyone who dreams dreams the beach.
For a while dead-ends are in vogue. For a while
open, uncharted cities. Years go by and all we've done is stare
at the ocean from one end of a mile-long lane
with our human eyeballs subject to the brain's commotion.
This was my boyhood, if you cared: the long
sweet coastal glide to paradise. Babinski raking his father's
field with a sprained wrist, endless ears of corn
left on the cornstalk firing out of their husks almost
edible. Memory Lane also mystifies: the sun
dwindling in a stream, me rewinding some hopeful words:
"Remembering is nice": and all the early anger
leaks out of my heart: then and now, home and boyhood:
there was a time that was enough to make
my head spin: reading another old stiff scanning the surf
for his floating face: same thought, same forms
of thought following their accidental beeline, like the few
undying oystermen taking a detour to the tavern
off Sagg Road, where the door's always dark, the sky still blue.

# Wild Hogs

The whole coast within eyeshot.
     I can count the ribs of the ocean—
Caribbean blue, Atlantic green,
     Caribbean blue—and patches of hillside
wild hogs have stripped. "Look
     away," says the hill, covering her face,
soaping her cheeks with a cloud.
     But I'm human and can't help myself
any more than hogs can. I go on
     looking at the bright bathers as they step
out of the ocean to towel off
     with their bright, Testarossa red towels
like God's laughter. It all starts
     with shame and want, I think, and ends
in shamelessness and want not.
     I can stand here so still a cicada might
mistake me for a stump and stab
     my bare leg to its bare heart's content.

## From a Middle Distance

At this moment I'm sitting in the sun
leafing through a book
on Velázquez with a pithy line
about his having painted mankind
because he couldn't see angels.
Exuberant, out of style, its Edwardian
era prose makes me blush,
eighteen again and gut-struck by ideas
I've just discovered in art
house films. I called movies *films*
back then. My labored hyperbole
put most people to sleep.
Now lunch is meager: steamed
asparagus, a glass of lemon water.
I'm learning to suck wind—
an old phrase of my father's
who'd drop words like *copacetic* with a wink
standing under a windmill
in tennis whites scuffed with clay
where he'd fallen during a match.
It's funny to see the bare trees
stunned out of their comas
by this unseasonable January
mopping the yard in lambent apricot
strokes, or watch snowmelt
disappearing in creeks
that politely disappear in the river.
Everything appears equally important

if all of it's to be gotten over:
ideas, styles, and incidents
of greater impact, which are personal
and therefore alone in me
translating into a yellowish morbidity.
"Speak well of me,"
says my father, and I offer
only knotted phrases that do not speak,
digging further into the book's
detail of *Las Meninas:* the narrow
face of a rousing mastiff
whose dark narrow eyes betray
knowing, which is to say restraint.

# Forgetting Waukesha, Remembering St. Helena

Forget the evenings of Slivovitz and sloe berry.
Forget drawing the immemorial
off-white latch. Forget willows on the banks
and the willow slips from whence.
All that you try with your mouth can be summoned:
boats the family sank by chopping
holes in the hull when they couldn't afford
Hoover's levy and children resorted
to rides on the dumbwaiter to spirit those prolonged

Wisconsin winters. At Napoleon's funeral,
a young foot soldier tried fitting on
the emperor's hat, hoping to spring to life
for the lachrymose officers and ladies
gathered in cool St. Helena. Having homage
and well-meaning mime in mind.
They were, after all, shutting Napoleon
inside four coffins as if he'd breathe like a potato.
It had that solemn air of the ridiculous,
you know, the soldier not getting his hat on square.

Momentarily he's my young father
refusing to break the news he's been laid off
and lay the groundwork for divorce. It's difficult to explain.
The mind rehearses, playing dress-up with a life.
He cannot hook the woman, his pinkies trained
perpendicularly. A vintage dress shirt slips from the line.
Pulling away in the middle of a dance, dancers become
movement on a floor—off-white, chamois. In his silence,
who is she, closing her eyes, four strands of her boy's hair
combed purposefully aside, allowing the white
of her raincoat to mask him? Mother, wife, coat.
She arches her back to receive his despondent head.
She puffs up her small breasts. Soft music's at work again,
a stereo plays "Love is Tender," romancing the age.
For six months my father dressed for work and wandered
no one will ever know where, Hotel Kempinski, say,
where he sat mutely in the plush barber's chair
dreaming he was as tall and modern as Peter the Great.

# Flywheel with Variable Inertia

*Home of Deanna Durbin*
*Home of Eddie "Rochester" Anderson*
*Home of Cary Grant . . .*

Like dreamy memento mori
little photos of each actor float
above each home in the picture postcards
tinged fraying sunset, tinged
bird of paradise, set in frames
and hung among "Hollywood's Treasures"
in the Los Angeles County
Library Annenberg collection
next to Chinese menus and crate labels
advertising citrus fruit—
California's "Second Gold Rush."

We live so strangely, in love with visions,
scared of the invisible. Once,
driving down a hill in Los Feliz,
I saw water rocket up twenty-five feet
out of the concrete at the busy
intersection below. Firemen ditched
their fire trucks on the corner;
they could only watch and coach
each of us through that airborne
bother of water, hoping we'd use caution
till the water wound itself down
or some brainiac from the DPW

devised a scheme to plug the hole—they couldn't,
after all, close traffic—and from
the top of the hill every car tipped
toward the water's pearly drywall
then paled and vanished
beneath a tumble of water, the train of us
cabled like rollercoaster cars
yahooing our lungs hoarse with the doors
locked and the windows rolled.
Then you were deep in it.
You had to squint to see the brake lights
of the guy ahead of you, whispering
the same prayer you whispered
to make it over to the other side.
What a pleasure on the tongue
saying "Rancho Cucamonga."

The city that had its way with us,
that wound us on its laugh track, where is it
going? Oceans of lime-colored
puffage are adrift, yet an actress cups her mouth
when she spots me blowing smoke
trying to create something
in a Hollywood courtyard
out of the stillness of that courtyard
the leaves of banyans cover.
Wigged and wingèd movie stars.
Arroyo willow jutting up from tar pits.
La Brea's redundancy of dire
wolf bones scooped from the mud
and posed in a mise-en-scène—

hunters frozen in that suck of heat.
I must look a little like death
fixing his spell over the turquoise trim,
smiling his odd smile at the feast
of ailments, dancing his danse macabre . . .
Just once I'd like to end up
on the other side of gravity, on varying
inversions of water—circuitous, coasting,
making its way up the winding stairs.
*Here we are in Ocean City, Here we're in Beloit*

# American Window Dressing

Half a dozen *pestemals* hanging on hooks,
       a cuckoo clock twigged from scrap metal,
a single copy of *Everyman's Haiku*—
       the letters pit the cover's look-at-me
moon sheen—and the poems I love
       inside: spartan, semitransparent, nature's fools,
like faraway countries in full disclosure.

"Put everything into it." My father's
       words on Sunday visits. Man of few words.
Those were the days work took him
       as far as Chungking and he sported
a straight green army coat he called
       his Mao Suit. His hair was still parted
straight to one side and he could

still lift me up so that I stood eyelevel
       with row after row of ducks, like smokers'
lungs, in the restaurant windows
       off Confucius Plaza—thick tar up top
swizzed into brown and rose gold.
       A metal sling dug under their wings
ended in a hole the heads were put through.

Knowledge of them was terrible.

     Everything looked terrible: more heads
of bok choy noosed in rubber bands

         and pale-eyed fish laid out on ice. Terrible
things put delicately, like polite fictions

         families invent. The words stand behind
great portals and are seen, yet untouchable.

# Rock Maple, White Pine

Part of you is thinking this early
why *ravel* means entangle and disentangle

at the same time, as if the interrogative
mood were the only concept

hanging about to hold the hour still.
In either hand, the frayed ends of conceit:

Frost cakes the pumpkin skulls.
Dirt and snow spiral upward off the steps.

From one room you stare into another—
seeing what you'd like to stick,

too much to puzzle out a single life.
Behind you, maple bark grows dull;

green-veined leaves are cinder at their edges.
Say it: the tree is sick. Love is far

from you. And you fix on the clear
sap of the petiole still

a season from rising, like potential
your mother saw in your father's

rhetorical Macedonian forehead
("Actually, it's Dutch").

No one could exceed her
childhood's silver sauceboats, the cheval glass

she tossed her dress in front of
like something out of Thomas Eakins.

Yet you catch yourself, remembering
process amounts to truth, the way

your father said, "Takes work
to eventuate a harvest," quoting

Whitman, you think, wishing he'd made
the same mechanics clear

to the young woman before she became
your mother. "Takes work"

so you confess you've just returned
from Philadelphia

and in your bored mind fin de siècle
reality appears firmly at hand:

cedar pegboards, table swifts, tilt-tops

built by Anabaptists
concerned with mortise and tenon,

not fumbling for abstracts
just the thumbprint

they say is from God. Logs to you
are trade for boards, and history

proves your German ancestors,
before they were Germans, settled here

for flax, sugar beets, and sorghum;
wheat old farmers called
the talismanic word; goose shanks

smoked three days or duck wing
brined in plunge blood;

"Where there's manure,"
they agreed, "there's Christ."

—Strangely enough you find yourself relieved
your world is set in the Midwest

and facts belong to this poem:
how Chenequa got its name from the Potawatomi
word for white pine, and 97% of its residents

descended from Bavarians,
Alsatians, Kashubians, Poles, "the wild Irish geese
of Erin," and Norwegians who died
so rapidly after an outbreak of cholera in 1851

graves were kept open
for corpses-to-come. One of the Schuette clan
departing for Manitowoc
wrote to explain the tears at Old World farewells:

" . . . anyone leaving for America
was considered as about to pass into eternity."

—Yet to come clearly out of the sumac
into the intentions

of nature, or begin in
philosophy's white pines and climb down

to sumac, is to act as if
you were a forester whose hand wasn't

resting on the spine of a book
about the first French traders and rapporteurs

traveling in flotillas
up the St. Croix, naming this spot Pointe de

Pomme de Terre, and that one
Prairie du Chien, scalloping the Chippewa

word for Wisconsin
which meant *great rock* or *gathering waters.*

Various tribes dovetail in the rising winter.
Coasts of trees, a noon sun

glorifying swamp grass. Your mind
mounts the old image of you

before you were this humor of replication
drawing the weather

out there from inside
and tempts you to mention how you feel

being a time-comprehending creature:
Snowdrift yields lament

or how in the grace light of morning
you jostle alive.

God some days, on others
records only, objects in history's logbook:

what in the end we ate, drank,
jarred, girded, anchored and housed.

# Hunchback

FROM THE ITALIAN OF ALDA MERINI

On morning's shore,
palm by palm, I watch the day rise
from the gray surf
and expressionless look of things.

My day means work;
the two shores refuse to touch.
I cannot dissolve into life, either
. . . no one helps.

But sometimes a hunchback idles by—
a sign of coming charity—
carrying the strange prophetic gift.

If I go out to meet my promise,
he will ferry me on his back.

## "what do you do?"

FROM THE ITALIAN OF EDOARDO SANGUINETI

what do you do? (they often ask): I say nothing back
    (sometimes): or else
I say instead (sometimes): nothing:
                            other times I say: too much, to
                            be honest
(but nothing that matters: and nothing that matters to me):
    (considering that,
shilly-shallying, nothing matters to me): (I'm merely following,
    often times,
this hushed hush-hush of a whisper whirring inside me, weakly,
    no longer even
turning into word, phrase, verse):
                            I seek an end in the end:

## "I taught my sons"

FROM THE ITALIAN OF EDOARDO SANGUINETI

I taught my sons to know my father was an extraordinary man:
    (they can
tell it like that, to someone, hopefully, in time): and then, that all
men are extraordinary:
        and that of a man there remain, oh,
about ten phrases, maybe (adding it all up: the tics,
the memorable remarks, the gaffes):
        and those are the lucky ones:

## "one writes especially"

FROM THE ITALIAN OF EDOARDO SANGUINETI

one writes especially because someone else may write, I said
to one of my children, the other day, and later: (because by now
   we're kind of trying
to write the complete works of humankind, all of us, together,
   deep down):
        and then
I related all of this to another of my children, another day, and
   this other child of mine
told me: that's how it should be:
            and then, yesterday, this same child told me
            one lives
especially because, etc.: (we were swept up in a great seaside
   roar on the Corso Italia,
in the night, above the beach, in a place called "Domenico's," I
   think):
(and I don't think I said anything back):
            (and then, see, my dear child, put
            that way, the thing
becomes too trivial, too tremendous, etc.):
            (and then, dear children, yesterday I
            gave
this other child of mine, mentioned above, before, a
   tremendous smack—for love):

# Rain

FROM THE ITALIAN OF EUGENIO MONTALE

Rain. A steady drizzle.
No motorbikes
backfiring or babies
crying.

Rain
from a cloudless
sky.
Rain
on these listless
hours of general
strike.

Rain
on your gravestone
at San Felice
at Ema.
No earthquakes
or war
shake the earth.

Rain
not on the lovely
long-ago fairy tale
but on the tax

form,
rain on cuttlefish bones
and bureaucrats.

Rain
on the Official Gazette
here from the wide balcony
rain on Parliament,
rain on Via Solferino,
rain with no wind
ruffling the cards.

Rain
God willing
in Hermione's absence
rain because absence
is universal
and if the earth isn't shaking
it's a sign Arcetri
didn't call it down.

Rain on the new epistemes
of the biped primate,
on deified man, on humanized
heavens, on the noses
of theologians in black tie
or workpants
rain on the lawsuit's progress
rain on work-in-regress
rain
on cypresses

sick in the cemetery, a trickle
on public opinion.

Rain yet where you appear
it's neither water nor vapor.
Rain, since if you're not here
it's just absence
and can drown.

# Westerly

Even up close it's hard to tell
whether the white and blue
church tower is defunct or half-finished
or, like every third house
block after prim block, let for summer.
Only an odd patch of moss
flecks the siding, and thin ginger-colored
stains make a noncommittal
braid, like wicker or wings at rest.
From our third-floor window
long scarves of water push
right up against the houses.
They seem to clip the gutter spouts.
If one were Elizabeth Bishop
one might hear it turn into a tidy music.
Tidy and resolved, the way
history says, "Look West, Future-looker,"
and kids worry a blue vein
of hope in their spiral notebooks.
At night after each boat has pulled in
behind the artificial bulwark
moonlight saddles a galvanized tub
of orange marigold and sedum,
and green and burgundy rosettes

creep upward like weird insect antennae
trucking the earth off to Westerly,
Rhode Island, where nirvana is a long time
coming, or untidy, unresolved,
the way stupid hope won't shut up.

## Beauty Spot

Those hills, maybe, at the bookends of summer.
Green bench in a shade, the Georgica jetty, magnificent ocean
rocks we hiked between. California wildflowers.
Some views of Grenoble going up the St. Hillaire du Touvet
funicular coupled with the knowledge that way
down there a poor half-Polish farmhand grew up to be the
    Eighth
Wonder of the World. Roberto sat in the same
spot by the Arno every afternoon for a year with a broken heart.
Later, he met his wife there. So now that place
in his mind is crossed with pain and happiness, which in many
people's books make beauty. Like staring out
at the gulf of Populonia while feeling the Etruscan necropolis
at your back. It's lovely to see, anyway: suddenly
lilies where lilies vanish, what house our earnest eyes conceive.

# Dante's House

Even after his death he did not return
to the city that nursed him.
—ANNA AKHMATOVA


After so much flame and high water,
the piazza's like a quarry sucked dry
when he returns, puzzling over an arch
window framed in fifteen-hundred
or so, after Orange leveled Florence
with cannon fire and the Guelph dead

iced up in their granite bas-reliefs.
He mistakes the number on the door
for an old friend's, yet his knock
fails to draw the familiar *Venga.*
He thinks: Are the banished past recall?
In his pocket a ring of keys turns up.
            One fits.

"*E' permesso?*" he asks, casting
a tube of light inside the room.
Vague recognitions wreathe the hall.
He hangs his crown of laurels up
and wiggles both his flatheels loose—
the floorboards are cool underfoot.

# Crenellated Playroom

*For Laura Rothenberg, 1981–2003*

Believe me it's late and I'm off on allusions
again, the involute recourse to layer
and meander, but it's come to me now,
the remark Elizabeth Browning made
after seeing Petrarch's study, as Italian redshirts
trumpeted by the Casa Guidi window
she was confined to staring from, and inside
her invalid body a few abstractions nagged—
love, justice, freedom—in a percussive
rehearsal of possession from the *piano nobile*,
which is really to say I am coming around
to my own subject, scaled down and grout
raked to the odd memorial detail of an old friend
assembling cuts of tile in her apartment
before her lungs collapsed; *And didn't it
move you*, wrote Browning, *the sight
of that little room where the great soul exhaled itself*?

—At her sickest, whittled down to brutal
humor only have-nots possess, grand dame
receiving guests in bed, Laura would say,
"That coat's really not your color" or "I hope
*she's* not at my funeral." I didn't drop by
the city often enough after Laura had left
the Bronx hospital to live with her boyfriend
in a one-room loft downtown, catty-corner
to St. George's Ukrainian Catholic Church
with its chipped Byzantine facade and globular
heaven dome the drunks outside McSorley's
mistook for a mosque, everything bundled
into the shape of their anger, before
heading back to the pub where wishbones
turned into a lintish slurry on a string
above the bar. Laura's body was rejecting
her new lungs. "To hell with living
through nightshifts on a stranger's watch,"
she said, she'd already willed her way
out of adolescence once. Her midlife crisis
peaked in prep school. Yet from the ceiling,
her family hung the same origami
cranes that dangled in every hospital room
—Kettering, Cabrini, St. Vincent's—
she knew as a child. I almost forgot
she was still a child, hearing the defibrillator
thump against her chest or watching her
haul around an oxygen tank while in-home
nurses coached her through the huff
cough or endlessly pounded her back to free
mucus clots, making me think momentarily

the drum is truer than the tremulous horn.
Out on the terrace, she laid tiles
for a table mosaic ("the denouement of the drama
queen," she laughed). China, seashell, smalto,
glass—the table was an upheaval of form,
like the crenellated battleground, our playroom,
where my brother and I once staged wars,
detonating action figures with our two mouths
ka-booming through the tiny apartment
and dragging our mother from her writing
desk. Her papers flew. Down the hall
she came screaming, "What happened in here?
What the hell have you done to your room?"

—The drum, yes, is truer than the tremulous
horn: insistent, instant, though with great beauty the horn
journeys out in front, panting to life,
an intermittent elision, steadying itself on the rail
of the drum, a weak creature crutched
by a strong. Mid-November and my last visit:
waiting in the hall, wanting to go
back to the pastoral flatland college
I'd come in from, settling to stand on the terrace
and face the cityscape with its storage
vaults and new cancellation in the sky,
some broken windows boarded, most buildings
rebuilt, the rough alto of drills and boom
operators luffing their load to the penthouse.
Motioning to the half-finished mosaic,
I asked, "When do you glue it all together?"
"As if," she said, employing the two small words
that acted as proxy for *no* in our time
and twisting me into her next cruel joke.
Yet there was no anger in her voice,
just, for a moment, an exasperated clarity,
as if she had no intention of seeing the work set
and was freeing me to imagine her
morning after morning yanking her thin cord of air
out to that table, steady and indomitable
as a 16th c. Italian servant approaching
a credenza, the buffet sideboard called belief,

referring back then to the act of testing
food for belladonna before expanding to contain
the room where the action unfolded,
and later the particular sideboard, what we
now call any old table we want to lift into hog heaven.

## Strange Giraffe

Perspective, put one way, is invitation to accident:
Andrea Del Sarto painting a strange giraffe
in the entourage of the Magi having only read
about giraffes in travel books, tired, maybe,
of the materials his time allowed, and hoping
an old spirit would stretch into the clothes of the living.

Me, I wake up to the city of bread and lilies,
inside a cenaculum, a penny wedged in each eye,
still wondering why the elaboration isn't harmless,
hunting for the long-ago life in my own life
and finding a mistake is the light behind the wattle.

Seeing the elephant once meant to see from
high perspective. The past, in hindsight, appears
clearly, riddled with wrong measurements:
elongate arms, a sun describing orbits around earth.
Out in the square, someone clears his throat
to phone home: "I can hear you, can you hear me?"

## A Kind of Poetry

Sometimes you turn to poetry
the way you turn to another country.
Everything is better. More humane.
You notice things you wouldn't
otherwise. You notice things.
Watching gardeners trim
branches for birds to fly through
reminds you of holes in your own country's trees,
which only make room for wires.
The entire center perforated
like a dart board in a dive bar.
After a while, however, you recall
those wires carry a language you know.

# The Farther Veil

They served fish at the fisherman's wedding—
*bianchetti*, catshark, turbot—
treasures the fisherman had trapped
and hauled in from the Gulf of Genoa.
What was meant to be sold abroad
he offered to his Japanese bride.
Her cream gown had been stretched
to fall around the child
kicking in her skirts.

For a month her mother had worried:
Will the girl give birth
before she is a wife?
She had caught the discomfort
her son-in-law masked
when she arrived alone at their house—
too skinny, looking poor.
When she made them dinner,
he shoved aside the length of eel
and ate plain rice. Her daughter
laughed and kissed him
on the mouth and spoke into his ear.

A day after the wedding, the groomsmen
walked the mother down to the port
and through the market.
By the fish stands she tried to show them
how to pick sea bream—the esteemed *orata*—

and slice it live for sashimi.
Once cut, its parts are put back together.

Her own seaside town had once been
thick with men; Januaries
they would walk naked to the shore,
naked save for mustard cloths
hugging their scrotums,
and together they would carry
a long, warped bamboo spear with delicate
white paper knotted on each end.
Only so many young men
could wield it, walking out into
the sea to set the paper on fire.
Their pale skin burned the naked eye.
These days young men skipped town.

Her hands failed to tell her story.
She found the eyes of the groomsmen
soft, weak, the color of cod buried in salt.

There are places where the sea goes dark
and the fish take off their scales.

"Push me there," she said, motioning
out of her purple bargain chiffon gown.

# Breughel in Rome

For the first few days, he picked fights with the cardinals. "What have you done with the farm girls, the fatboys straddling wine casks?" He tried explaining beauty. "Putti come to life," he said, "if you just break their wings." He packed the Tempietto with riffraff. After a while, he threw up his arms. The cardinals went away, convinced they'd met another Franciscan. Up late sobbing on the phone: "How did I end up here? Where are the girls who get around on ice skates?" When he finally left, he made the driver draw the curtains in his carriage. "So much for heaven," he said, putting a bit of distance between himself and the interior, where little boys in that country noose geckos with blades of grass . . .

I'm recording this on the couch in nothing but a Dolphins sweatshirt. It's nearly 7. The sun is making pink on the Atlantic, and my neighbor's dachshund is barking his balls off at the first signs of life. I've sucked down half the juicebox my wife picked up last night. I hope, by saying this, I can pre-empt those questions students always ask when they're bored or at a loss: the time, the day, what hand I hold my pen in, wherever the hell I was when something happened into my head. Circumstance isn't a total wash; you can sort of be anywhere, I tell them, and you sort of can't. Music is essential. Some kinds of looking. Like, you want to look so hard the whole country goes to pieces.

# Apparitions and Incarnations

—After my father died I grew *great* ~~my father's beard~~. I could carry him
around with me and not some
hunger to be my own man.
The sky shut. Inside it shut the mountain.


—Maids when their masters passed them
used to turn to face the wall
so their masters could stroll on
in the heavy accumulation of their suits
believing magic kept house.


—Life withdrew into its ordinary enclosure;
on TV, Gonzo swam in a rubber
Nixon mask. I remember being told
what the world felt like then
and felt it was familiar—unmoored, arch.


—Possession's a sort of sad business;
even the gods can't win an audience in their own
skins, can neither confuse themselves
with their vessels nor forget they must
step off the stage to fulfill the seduction.

## Louise's Story

I like that squirrel and his idiot dance up the tree.
I like that tree hanging wide a little leftward.
One sad-looking thing making another something happy.
Sometimes it's just us ruffling the leaves.
Sometimes I find myself inside the soiree of a woman's hair,
not really caring, a little high on the ineffable.
Louise, in her late bouffant style, used to tower
tuna sandwiches with half a bag of Cape Cod
chips in her retirement. What was happiness to her
or she to happiness? 1986, New York, heading
uptown on the 6 train to her volunteer job at the Met.
One year she had her taste of it. Sometimes
joy is no affair of oblivion. Sometimes a purchase on its limbs is got
by a great act of will. Yet maybe her whole story,
how it's been told to me and how I've read
between what I've been told, is merely several
platforms of imagination, that shunting faculty that props
a scaffold on the face of things and says *Beware*.

# Elba Journal

Heat in the tent, hard ground. I hang my arms
out the opening for a drop of air
until a heave of flies drives me back in again
and I lie still for a sleepless hour.

It's easy to imagine giving up, like Rimbaud.
The brain quits braiding its elaborate
elocutions. The past is around us but isn't
pressuring or insufferable. My journal

fills with sea lily and holly. On my way to piss,
I spy a boy swallowed in the husk
of his hammock. The spirit, though we make it
otherwise, isn't complicated, rising
and falling in its calligraphic exhaustion.

## After *A Silvia*

*Mirava il ciel sereno,*
*Le vie dorate e gli orti,*
*e quinci il mar da lungi, e quindi il monte.*
—GIACOMO LEOPARDI


Remember? You used to thumb
through the pages of *Seventeen*
eyeing each snapshot of other
girls on the slopes of girlhood.
The song you sang at school
drifted through the quiet rooms
and out the street. Vague, whatever-will-be,
May took up the air. I dropped
my books. I shoved my papers in a drawer—
half my life sewn shut inside
my father's house—and cupped my ear
to catch the sound of your voice
as you hauled your heavy workload home.
I'd look out at the clear sky,
the bright streets, people's yards,
all the way down to the sea
and all the way up the hillside.
No words really fit what I felt.
The hopeful pitch of then.
To think of that time tightens my chest
and grief ploughs through me.
Shock and blowback, tricks and masks—

why is it nothing keeps its word?
What's with all the lights burning in the distance?
Before winter starved the grass
or some compliment was paid
your modest, nothing-special looks,
some narrow sickness buried you.
Whatever boyhood I had
fate hijacked too. Old friend, is this that
world we stayed awake all night for?
Truth dropped in. Far off,
your cool hand points the way.

# Notes

The book's epigraph is excerpted from "A Reply to Matthew Arnold on My Fifth Day in Fano," from *Above the River: The Complete Poems*, by James Wright, introduction by Donald Hall. Copyright © 1990 by Anne Wright. Reprinted by permission of Farrar, Straus and Giroux, LLC.

"Golden State Sublet": The line in italics appears in Jack London's *John Barleycorn*.

"Transparent Window on a Complex View": The poem takes its title from a remark made by Fairfield Porter in *Art in Its Own Terms: Selected Criticism, 1935–1975*.

"From a Middle Distance": The book mentioned in the opening lines is James Huneker's *Promenades of an Impressionist*.

"Rock Maple, White Pine": Whitman is actually quoted as saying, "Even when [Emerson] falls on stony ground he somehow eventuates in a harvest" in *With Walt Whitman in Camden*, vol. 3, by Horace Traubel. The poem is also indebted to *The History of the John Schuette Family* by Edward Elhert; *From Farmland to Freeways: A History of Waukesha County, Wisconsin*, edited by Ellen Langill and Jean Penn Loerke; and *Pine Lake* by William F. Stark.

"Hunchback": "Il Gobbo" is Merini's first published poem, written when she was seventeen. It appears in *Fiore di Poesia*, copyright © 1998 Giulio Einaudi editore S.p.A, Turin.

"what do you do?" / "I taught my sons" / "one writes especially": All three poems appear in *Mikrokosmos: Poesie, 1951–2004*, copyright © 2004 Giangiacomo Feltrinelli Editore, Milan, Universale Economica series.

"Rain": The original poem, "Piove," appears in *Satura, 1962–1970,* by Eugenio Montale, copyright © 1971 Arnoldo Mondadori Editore S.p.A., Milan.

"Dante's House": The epigraph is from "Dante," *Poems of Akhmatova,* translation © 1973 by Stanley Kunitz with Max Hayward (Mariner Books, Houghton Mifflin Harcourt).

"Crenellated Playroom": Browning's letter appears in the second volume of *The Letters of Elizabeth Barrett Browning*, 1897 (Macmillan).